# In Love

# In Love

## Veronica

It all began on March 23, 2023.

I felt a kick and a heart beating with warmth.

I knew it couldn't be.

# CHAPTER 1

## Beyond March 23

He was not even a fetus yet but I could feel him in the bottom of my baby sac. He would beat as though as it had already been 3 months pass. Then, he would be silent and still, but still warm in my baby sac.

Tonight, he called out in my mind

~ Mother, I love you.

Then,

~ Mother, may I have some water? Some Arrowhead room temperature water?

I quickly went to the kitchen and patiently took a plastic bottle of Arrowhead water from the pantry. I drank slowly and deliberately, as though, he felt it trickling onto him and nourishing him.

Then, he communicated,

~ Mother, may I have some Sunkist orange? The one you brought from the table into your desk.

With assurance, I felt his thirst for the freshness of the orange (God created the trees with the fruits), I peeled the orange with my fingers pressing my thumbnail into the skin.

After I was done, always thinking of him, I squeezed open the orange into two halves. Delectably, I ate. . .he liked it.

I was in love.

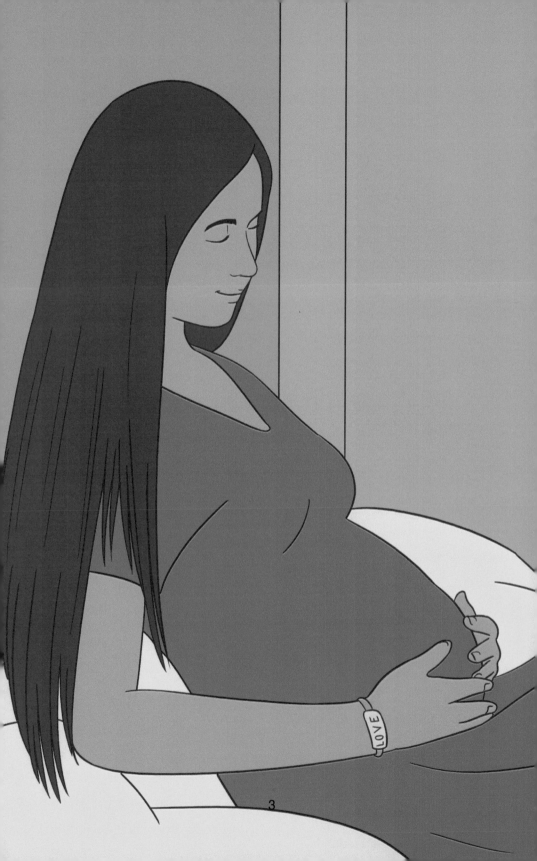

# CHAPTER 2

## In Love

As his love coursed through my body, in my blood vessels, the love of God came to mind. Unusual though it may be, this love did not want to stop in my vessels. My skin remained youthful. It became to glow, others told me. My hair grew long, and black and silky. Silky, literally silky as the silk from the finest silk worms in China. My nails became glossy and shiny. I cut them clean and short enough to show 3 millimeters of the white part. The other parts of my senses and bodies lived in a similar way, as he grew in my baby sac.

All the time, I thanked God for this love, love of my child-to-be. Now, 3-months.

5

# CHAPTER 3

## In Love Even More

How could anyone be in love even more?? But, I was. In my baby sac, as he grew, the world changed.

He communicated that people around me were nicer.

They were kinder. They greeted, 'hello', very often. They nodded in appreciation of my baby sac. It goes on.

As the communication lessened, just the thought of knowing him was enough to warm the fire of love in my entire body. I coaxed myself, wanting. He was resting and cuddling in my baby sac - sleeping no doubt. I could not wait until I felt him again, and the way he just communicated in my mind . . . warm.

The warmth would keep me comfortable in 42 degrees' temperature in the room. It was the feeling of champurrado- a warm tasting dessert that I always have a craving for.

The warmth lighted up the night sky outside like fireworks on New Year's Day. Outside, it was dark because it was 4:59 a.m., but I could see the light, radiating out from the socket of my eyes.

# CHAPTER 4

## It Is All About Feeling

At 4 months, he was big in my baby sac.

He pictured in my mind how he'd be, suckling on my breast; then older he was, playing with a common clown colored beach ball; then older he became, keeping a secret of the adventures that would take place in his life.

This was too quick for me. As he was in my baby sac, I felt I said

~ Remain in me for as long as needed

~ I will carry you and fill your thirst with water and quench your appetite with fresh oranges

~ Remain in me and you and I will be together, forever. . .

for 9-months, anyway.

# CHAPTER 5

## Positive Vibes/Vibrations

At 7 and a half months onwards, I could feel his physical movement in my sac.

It was like an alien moving around. I didn't know what to expect but I loved. And, I could see the little fists and feet moving just under my tummy.

The positive vibes began to exude. The rain these days helped the recovery from the drought; the bright lights became the (blinding) light for Christ; the air smelled of fresh cut grass; the friends became closer physically around me; the hugs became dear; the food became most fragrant and delicious; just everything seemed to be right.

# CHAPTER 6

## The Baby

At 9 months, he came. The promise has been fulfilled.

Milton Keynes UK
Ingram Content Group UK Ltd.
UKHW051407261123
433239UK00001BA/5